NATIONAL GEOGRAPHIC

T0040049

How Are Magnets Used?

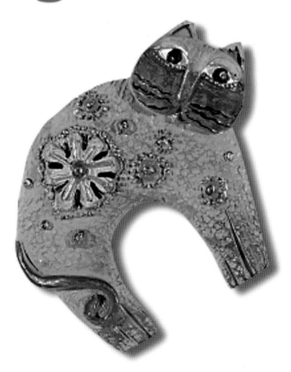

Jan Pritchett

Magnets

Magnets are used for lots of different things.

Magnets can stick to some metals. They can be used to stick, or hold, things together.

Magnets are used all around us.

MAGNETS

Game Boards

This checkerboard is made of metal.
There is a magnet in each checker.
The magnets in the checkers stick
to the board.
The magnets keep the checkers
from falling off the board.

Refrigerator Doors

To keep things cold, a refrigerator
door must close tightly.
There is a magnetic strip around
the door.
The magnetic strip sticks to the
metal frame of the refrigerator.
The magnet keeps the door
closed tightly.

Message Boards

A message board holds
information for people to read.
The message board is made
of metal.
Magnets stick to the metal board.
The magnets hold the papers
in place.

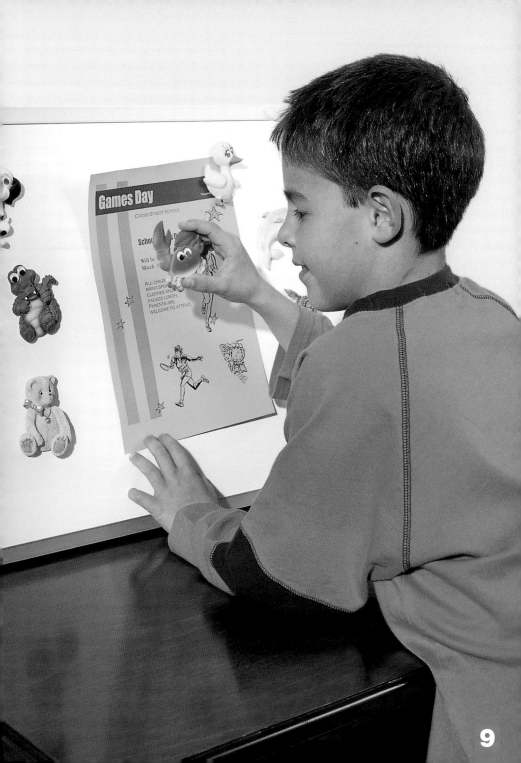

Toy Trains

This toy train has cars that
move together.
Each train car has a magnet at the
front and the back.
The magnets stick to each other.
The magnets keep the train
cars together.

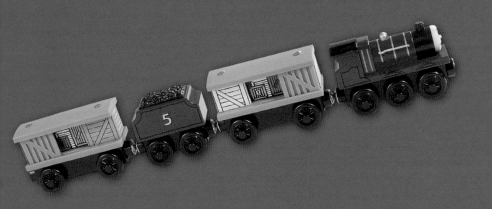